Her parents and fourteen kids
rode in a rumbling farm wagon,
rode fifty grieving miles
to level land close to creeks.
Nobody knew these strangers.

Mother wept bitter tears
remembering and telling
about those paper dolls.

SCARS STILL SHOW

A fat two-year-old baby
has legs badly bowed
from malnutrition, rickets—
or congenital reasons.
The bowing worsens.

His mother
carries the baby to a hospital
in the summer of 1912.
Two doctors struggle
while nurses nervously help.
The father wrings his hands,
the mother races through her rosaries.

The doctors break both legs
to straighten them.
The baby screams.
For five years
his legs wear horse-heavy braces.
While his mother works in the fields,
neighbor farm girls
rock his buggy
and sing German songs.

His legs grow straighter stronger.
But two miles to school
is too far;
the boy always falls behind,
out of breath.

As the boy grows up
his legs slowly heal.

A navy doctor asks him for details
makes him run in place
double time.
"You're in the navy, sailor."
His shipmates fuss,
"What's with those crosses?"

SOLDIERS COME

I crouch low
resting, dream
behind current bushes
hanging rich with red rosary beads.
Angry bees buzz,
swirl madly about.
I taste sour gooseberries,
the moment
lazy with peace.

Hearing a noise,
I hide
deep down and quiet
I hear
hut! two! three! four!
and see
men marching, shouting.
Some carry brooms,
others shoulder squirrel guns.

Hut! two! three! four!
They march in time
toward Little Chicago.

I crouch lower still,
crawl, then run.
Safe inside the house, I cry,
"Mama, Mama,
so many men
are walking stiff,
hollering loud."

"Yes, son.
They practice to go to war
to fight the Kaiser
in the old country."

"What's war, Mama?"

CLEARING LAND

In the far long ago
in the dark wooded north
my father was a lumberjack—
as others told it
a crackerjack of a lumberjack.

The lumberjacks felled giant pines,
sled upon sled of sky high logs.
Mules dug in their steel-shod toes,
whips cracked, hunkies cursed,
rocking loads creaked, swayed,
slid down riverbank roads.

It was dark before they ate
potatoes busheled on each plate
slabs of venison buried under onions.
A thousand beans on each man's platter
coffee by the hottest bucketful,
two-fisted slabs of sour apple pie.

Saturday nights at the saloons
were raucous swearing loud
everybody drank hard, whiskey
to forget the pain, to remember the absent.
Arms hooked together later in the night
they swayed, staggered to the bunkhouse.

My father never talked much about those
      times,
only smiled when one of his woods pals
said, "Remember when ..."
He never cursed any more—just nodded
toward the dark wooded north.

FOREVER MYSTERY

Forever runs the river
dark and deep, mysterious—
quiet, forever rushing
toward some unseen sea
sometimes churning fiercely
over angry rapids—
quiet again,
before roaring on
to fall
in swirling pools below.

Like my father
quiet, and deep, mysterious—
forever busy, hurrying
toward some unseen goal
seldom idle
relaxing only
with yellow corn cob pipe
thinking, always thinking
toward tomorrow, and tomorrow's
undone chores.

GO GENTLY WITH THE AX

The black kettle is boiling,
block and tackle are set,
scalding barrels steady.

"Crack hog skulls—
bang between the eyes
don't swing wild
—if you miss
the hog races away"

"Crack hog skull—
soon as pig drops
stick knife deep
middle above belly
bleed her good

String legs on hooks
pull hog high
dip in, dip out of barrel
drop her on platform
scrape hide clean
shave-whisker clean

Hang critter high
cut her open
spill guts in dishpan."

Short and tough
old Frank talks Low German
cracks bad jokes.

When he and Pa are done
they drink brandy,
claim booze
kills the killing taste.

UNDER WHERE ?

Before Playtex
mothers made bloomers
from unbleached
flour sacks.

Their sewing skills varied;
so did
the slap-dash bleaching.

Flour mill ads
warmed girl bottoms,
and stirred boy curiosity.

Big Jo bags
bragged:
Hasn't Failed Yet.

Here's what happened
to Nettie
in fourth grade—

emblazoned
across her ample rear,
Gold Medal's famed claim:
Eventually, Why Not Now?

CATACOMBS

Environmental concerns
are my life career—
to dig channels
to aerate and irrigate

My home is smelly dark
and pneumonia-damp
but it's home—
gardener came this morning
dull-edged hoe chopping
messing up my neighborhood

Cultivating garden he claims
planting dumb radishes
horrid onions
crooked carrots
expects me to live here

It's home, and a job.
Tomorrow this earthworm—

is going fishing.

A LOT OF BULL

When my parents went to town that noon,
he came for an uninvited visit.
I still see his rusty red coat.

My job was to herd the cows to water.
Usually there were stragglers,
but this day we had a huge visitor.

I was six years old and still not a yard high
(our cow-yard gates towered six feet).
Snorting, he glared down on me.

I am no Jack with his beanstalk—
giants still frighten me witless.

ETHNIC GARDENING

Plant only white beans with white—
belly buttons up on black ones

Keep pumpkins away from melons—
mixing varieties ruins both species

Stick the onions upwind from fennel—
even favored flavors don't blend

Snap suckers off tomato blooms—
mothers can only nurse so many kids

Keep neat crop rows, weed all plants—
shows the gardener really cares

Don't lean much on rakes and hoes—
nosey neighbors peddle petty gossip

REMEMBERING
100 BIRTHDAYS

Half a century ago
he was laid out
for family and neighbors
to nod their *Our Fathers*.

"Now he can really rest,"
they comforted.

On the twentieth of September
I am drawn back
to his grave on the hill,
greeting his 100th birthday.

I see again
his almost always tiredness—
asleep in his rocker
beside the warming oven
of our pale blue range.

I see again
a Sunday's buggy drive
to High Cliff for a balloon ride.
The balloon caught fire
and there was no ascent.

How could this numbers-smart
grade school dropout
help me fathom absurd algebra,
dark-sided geometry?
His mind never napped.

It's time, Pa:
now you should really rest.

CHICKEN SNOOP

Willie Wilson had a weasel face;
they said
he was a chicken thief.

Smiling, sneering,
Willie spooked neighbors' farmyards,
hunting for hickory nuts
he claimed.
Nobody believed him.

In the dark of a stormy night
folks heard
dogs barking,
commotion in the henhouse.
They feared weasels,
but they knew
Willie Wilson was fixing
to treat his boozing buddies
to a kettle of chicken booyah.

Pa swore he stole
the onions and potatoes too.
Weasel soup, Ma called it.

Willie Wilson is dead now,
choked on a chicken bone
the paper said.

THE DAY AFTER
JUDGMENT DAY

I brooded
in the cemetery.

Why was the name
on that tombstone
the same as mine—
the date,
yesterday's?

Troubled, brooding,
I stalked on home.

The phone was ringing;
a man said he was a mortician
asked why I had missed my funeral
yesterday.

I brooded again,
for the third time.
Finally, in relief,
it dawned on me:

in superstition,
as in baseball
three times is out.

I'm home free.

THE RAG MAN

The cold rumbles of World War II
cast their pall over Poland.
At his university, the shape of Moishe's nose
became a cause for concern
so he escaped
to the open-hearted bosom of America.

Where would he live and where
could bread be earned? Maybe toward
the middle of this promised land.

Wisconsin drew him,
opened its German gates; the rolling hills
and dales reminded him of back-home
Poland.

Learned Moishe bought a horse
to pull a big wagon, roaming
the countryside, buying rags
and sometimes iron.

He came to our farm each new season,
years and years of friendly business. We
saved faded old rags in worn burlap bags.

Moishe and his horse Maxey worked hard—
and fairly—to dig a dirty living
from the tired leavings of often unfriendly folk
who tried to twist an unkind joke
or cheat this gentle foreigner
among slightly-less-recent immigrants
who brought their hates here.

When Maxey died, Moishe got a teaching job at a university where he became again esteemed Professor of Economics.

POLICE CHIEF PRIM

He rode higher, stood taller,
this white-whiskered, white-haired lawman.
Well-groomed, distinguished, the press said.

But, under his elegant chin plumage,
he was rumored to carry crimeland scars
from 25 years on Chicago's police force.

He stayed a Chicago White Sox fan,
a rabid fan, friend of Comiskeys, with a
free annual pass to all Windy City games.

In Wisconsin, he rode a sleek black armored
     Buick
with a uniformed ram-rod driver up front—
the "Black Maria" proud citizens baptized it.

He was unsmiling, his men
claimed; he could wither the wayward
with a steely glare from under his bushy
     brows.

He rode higher, stood taller
astride his white parade horse.
Military erect, no-nonsense, law in-charge.

The city stood straighter, folks thought
right.
His manner and bearing, his expect-
ation, tugged us all higher and taller.

For 22 years he was chief of police here,
George T. Prim, Chief Prim please,
the white horse and the Black Maria.

A TASTE FOR DYNAMITE

Who knows the mind of a dog
running behind cattle
jogging beside horses?
Part Dalmatian, part foxhound,
busybody Tippy was
not quite half-wit.

Always tail-wagging,
bobbing his spotted head,
his six-inch red tongue
lapped lather.

Blasting stumps
was his wildest joy—
lit fuse fizzing
at a blasting stump hole
set Tippy barking crazily.
Then boom, in his silly face.

Who knew the mind of that dog
—if mind there was?
Often flash-blinded,
he never learned
or promptly forgot
the next time we blasted
again boom, right in his silly face.

WINTER'S WEEPING

Parade of winter crystals
diamond daggers
sun-catcher swords
melt dripping,
along roof-warmed eavelines.

To lick mid-winter's tongue-numbing,
I reach high for another
yard-long icy stalagtite.

Late afternoon,
the dripping slows.
One more five-foot glass-like lance
leaves its eave
crashes
shatters
pierces crusted snow mounds
lands
at my booted, chilling feet.

PLAIN TALK

Henry fixed cars
said the collecting rods
were shot
same with the
pistol rings
insisted
"she needs a new carbolator"
lucky
he fixed better
than he talked

Sophie went to church
daily
even weekdays
stayed for two Masses
scolded God
"be sure
you keep track
some day when I'm even more
old and crippled
I want credit
for when
I can't come no more."

God heard—
Henry's cars lasted
longer than he did
Sophie hit 97

WHOSE SHADOW
FOLLOWS ME?

Homebound after a horror movie
more than a mile still to go
city street lights half a mile behind,
farmhouse lights turned off hours ago
night black as the inside of Dracula's derby.

One lone hound dog howls
at whose moon I'm not sure—
Two huge shadows from behind
move first to right, then left.
Stretching,
they fall in front of me.

I know it futile to run.
I call out to the shadows:
"You going to Little Chicago?"
Through the black night
a low grim voice answers:
"Nope.—Going out to Lehrer's woods
to kill myself;"

I run track-meet fast, all the way home,
throw my jacket and pants on the floor,
hang my cap on the straight chair
at the foot of the bed,
pull blankets over my head.
But sleep never comes
until three in the morning.
I dream of shadows.

Day breaks just after four.
At the foot of my bed sits a stranger.
I never move a muscle, never breathe,
my heart pounds.
I pray he will go away.

Day's light comes slowly—
on the chair at the foot of my bed,
between me and breaking day's window,
hangs yesterday's shirt
and my own ragged cap.

I REMEMBER THE DAY
OF MY HANGING

They dumped that beat-up '29 Ford
in the purple shade of a sagging elm.
Grabbing pitch forks,
they roared off to stuff barley bundles
into that groaning Rumely monster.

They left the rumble seat
of that old roadster
yawning wide open.

Nobody noticed
the 40-foot bull rope swing
that dangled
from a high branch of the elm,
caressing the threshing dust
from the old Tin Lizzie.

The noon whistle shrilled—
engineers shut down their black
powerhouse,
Rumely's roaring
stopped with a grunt.

Belly-hungry bundle pitchers
raced for the Ford
and piled in.
I got the knee-cramping rumble seat.
The crazy-driving kid wheeled off
with an angry screech.

Nobody noticed
the rumble-seat passenger
nor the swinging bull rope
as it slid round the Ford's roof
looping briefly around my throat
smashing my skull
against the lip of the lid
of that rumble seat cover—
finally flipping off.

My neck still hurts.

HOW MANY TIMES . . .

now listen here Madame Hare
you and I know I have no right
to press the question of family size

and yet to beget and beget
without house or ready home—
to move in uninvited on others

now there must be sensible limits
on how many times you've settled here
— and parked new broods with us

my murmuring now is growing louder;
I've seen your hidden bassinet
waiting, ready for your confinement

down between two pea pod rows—
I'm counting on those crops you know
you have no right without invite

you circumvent my leaky fence
to dig and pad your birthing nest
you root around my yard and garden

the time has come world mother
for us to have an earnest chat—
deliver first, then by rights begone

and when we finally think we can
let's get you down to get new help
from Planned Parenthood for Rabbits.

WISE AND OTHERWISE

Harold, my skit partner,
had a withered left arm
but was never withered in his skull.
"Wise and Otherwise" was what
we tagged our one-liner act.

We were very funny.

Tipping our straw boaters
time after nervous time,
we scanned cue lines
pasted inside the hat tops.

And we were cheap—

most we ever collected
for forty wonderful minutes
was a buck-and-a-half apiece.

I can feel the stomping now,
and hear those raucous jeers again.

SELLING SHOES
IN SOUTH DAKOTA

My boss knighted me as foot-and-shoe
expert
sent me to dust-buried Dakota's badlands.

A tank of gas cost less than a dollar—
west winds howled, altering landscapes.

Skies turned midnight dark at noon,
hid highways under blackest blankets.

Blizzards of dust ripped up the prairie soils,
heaped anxiety on Depression's grim pain.

Double-header troubles roiled together,
spreading gloom over land and people.

Families huddled coatless and barefoot;
even the cheapest shoes stole absent dollars.

The firm's shoes, slightly orthopedic,
cost more than drifting acres of land.

One sale I remember. A stone deaf old-timer
barged in, hollering: "You gotta help me.

All my shoes crack open! When I pee, I don't
pee out, I pee down. Makes my shoes crack!"

Thank God for eager youth's blind naiveté,
thank God dinner cost only thirty-five cents.

MOUSE HOUSE

The empty lake cottage way up north
is ours for the spring holiday weekend
after four hundred miles of Friday driving.

Two tired out parents, two sleepy kids,
we hit the mattresses as soon as we arrive.
Tomorrow: boating, fishing, swimming.

Loons on the lake scream, and a
whip-poor-will calls near midnight.
The kids sleep, but I hear new noises.

In an oak chest at bed's head, a mouse runs,
banging tools over rusty handsaws,
squeaking his unwelcomed welcome.

I get up, set a baited trap in the drawer,
then back to bed before the trap
snares a whimpering mouse.

Now, a new night noise: mouse
dragging itself and trap
endless miles in oak chest drawer.
Will sleep ever come before daybreak?

Up with eager, rested kids. But first,
I roll the chest to the sheltered porch
where the mouse can live or die,
before exhaustion kills us all.

EDGE OF AWARENESS

Darkening stillness surrounds
a thousand trees standing
erect against the hard west wind
against autumn's chilling weather.
Trees listen to each other sigh,
wait for another lonely night.
Whispering leaves send signals
to the leaves of other trees—
wait for tomorrow's new light

Where the wood's edge meets meadow
an alone deer stands stiffly still.
Its alert ears are cupped forward, listening
to the echoes of unheard sounds
deep from the still dark forest—
watching for tomorrow's light

II

GIVE US THIS DAY

38

thank God
    it's still
        Friday

so many dreams
    unlived

so many joys
        unsavored

most challenges
        as yet unmet

so many tasks
        unfinished

thank God
    it's still
        Friday

give us this day
    again and
        again

MALLS AS THEATRE

Open air opera unfolds under glass
flutters with excitement
murmurs with musical noises.
A gathering of today's cast of thousands,
and a scattering of walk-ons
play out rituals, to preen and prance,
perchance to strut, to buy dish pans
or dress-up things? Dreaming the
glass slipper dreams, worrying about
the wrath of plastic credit gods.
There is religion being served here.
On stage everyone—music up,
lights bright, act your part.

A GRAIN
OF MUSTARD SEED

On a day in the Holy Season,
our minds full of prayerful reason,
the **good book** arrives.

Page after hopeful page
is full of promise and heavenly grace,
good cheer for earth's heavy-hearted.

Words and pictures stir yearnings,
encourage faith, prod action
so our tomorrows will overflow with beauty.

Bless the fruits of our goodness—
may the skies suckle our roots
as we devour the newest seed catalog.

*Appearing in AT WATER'S EDGE, anthology
of The National Library of Poetry, 1995*

WINTER'S HEEL

Neighbors notice his endless kneeling, the
peering deep into winter-pressed grasses.
He overhears their words of certain senility.
Their nervous draperies part noticeably:

> see now his foot-long flashlight
> his spying glass
> what is that aging codger hunting?

Those fussing worriers
what can they know
about spelling the magic of a stalled spring?

Would they see the inch-high hyacinth,
the tulip's promise, the peeking five wild
> violets;
a budding spring dandelion,
the unheard wiggling of earthworms?

SPRING CLING

There they were, arguing
about who would
finally
come home with whom

He wore his reddest vest
and she her spring bikini;
he was eager, and busy,
tugging at her torso

The more he dragged—
and pulled—
the more she resisted,
even more so

The grimmer he grew
the tougher he clung
the wearier she grew
the more certain she knew

Virtue must prevail—
prevail it shall;
her attacker now thinking
his eyes now blinking

Now with night falling
he feared the darkness—
how would he ever find
the wife he left behind

Off flew harassing robin
leaving behind virtue's torso;
Ms. Earthworm slithered home,
her earthly home—even more so.

IMPATIENT GARDENER

This morning I planted our early garden.
Between the pea pods and onions
—four hopeful rows of each—
I planted lettuce and carrots
with radishes snuck in.

By afternoon, I'm already alarmed.
Nothing's up in the garden,
just stakes to mark the rows
and pale green tops of thirty onion sets.

What are those lazy seeds thinking of,
down in their dark underground?
Gardening should be a growth industry,
but nobody told the seeds.

BIRDS IN A FIELD

His front bicycle wheel twirled
lazily in spring's breezes

(knee-high alfalfa hid the rest
of that crazily abandoned bike).

He sprawled nearby as if hurt,
leaning on one elbow, staring east.

I feared startling him from behind
so I edged around to his seeing side

and called gently to him. He turned.
I recognized my former neighbor.

He raised a work-worn finger to shush
my eager questions.

Holding up five fingers, he pointed
half-whispering, toward bluebirds:

"See the daddy on that far birdhouse,
he's hopping now to the perch in front,

telling his bride inside to stay
warming her eggs, to wait for his return."

Tree swallows swirled about, skimming
blooming legume blossoms, catching aphids.

He smiled at them, and then with a nod
called them "worthy birds" as well.

A DAY AWAY

Sixteen black ants
out-race my grasp
to crawl over, to chew
my dropped chicken wing
with sweet-sour sauce.

Between swaying green grasses
the tiny creatures operate factories
find food and shelter
build pueblo hill homes
maintain civilizations.

I study their way of living:
getting on with hurry-scurry
making ant love, burying their dead
building up, tearing down.
Welcome to my chicken wing.

FISH BIRDS

Seagulls, herring gulls, fish gulls
swirl, swoop, loop-the-loop,
screech, scream, dive-bomb,
alarming September's calm harbor.

Then they turn dumb—
eighty-nine gulls,
all shades of gray,
some with speckled bottoms,
the yearling young simply colorless,
the older gulls chalky white.

Call them terrorists. Or are they
simply survivors
of the fittest among the fit?

My smoked chub lunch done,
I toss what's left
of oily skins and fishbone skeletons
into the roiling, rocking waters
at harborside.
The gulls attack
in harshest seagull lingo.

Then, along sagging roofline ridges,
they line up
Indian file,
sideways
and wait.

Shifting from one leg to the other,
they move swivel-necked
to stare droopy-eyed
in deadlike silence.

CARDINAL IN BLOOM

In an earlier time this was a sandbox
where children played out their dreams—
building up and breaking down sand castles,
filling buckets and pails with smaller pails.

Today it blooms a crazy quilt:
cosmos, asters, petunias, zinnias, marigold.
Bumble and honeybees visit this nectar
garden
turning colors into honeycomb.

On Sunday a flitting flower moved about
among this field of exploding blooms.
Not an errant bouquet cast loose by breezes,
no—this was a nervous flaming red vision.

It hopped, skipped, flew from stem,
from stake to stalk, from nodding blossom,
back to a yellow marigold.
No windswept budding flower,
no—the ultimate fauna, this red bird
with the happy wolf-whistle, the girl-call song.

FLY ON MY WINDOW

Winter's harshness etched lacy castles
on opaque window panes
while I drifted in sleep last night.
When day's light climbed,
glistening the frosted castles,
out of one still-sleepy eye
I watched a staggering cold-drugged fly
skate and slide and slide
along the icy rink on my window.

I didn't swat the fly,
admired instead
its valiant try
at out-of-season survival.

How would I
struggle to cope
among the frozen fears
of wintery spires,
shivering in bone-chilled alarm
doubting
of ever again
being cozy and house-fly warm?

DESIGNER HORSE

monkeys may chatter chatter
but they don't have a smatter

where in dusty dry savannahs
do baboons hide green bananas

hyenas are the laughing stock
Rhodes scholars they are not

wacky jungle kid's computer
beeps the news: "zebra's cuter"

out with leopard's polka dots
out are tiger's crooked spots

zebra shows off jailbird stripes
simple study: black and white

you can lead a horse to water
but zebras you shouldn't oughter

SLEEPING AROUND

Snakes and mice shared my bed in the hay—
my dog-tired exhaustion from the threshing
    grind
soothed all fussiness about bed-fellows.

Fresh air fiends in Navy training halls
froze all sleep from my bunk and pillows.
A steam-heated laundry room bench saved me

from pneumonia while I dried sailor whites.
I've slept under apple trees at noontime,
resting up for scorching field work

after back-breaking hours of endless crop toil.
I've slept alone beyond the drape where
a heavy-breathing woman assumed I lay
    awake.

Late night banjo-plucking left me drowsy
during my five-in-the-morning milking chores
—until a nervous cow kicked over my pail.

I've slept with the same woman more than
fifty years, never deciding for sure who
snored most or loudest.

Appearing in FOX CRY in 1995

RUB THE PENNY

Mr. LeRoy, blind since Viet Nam,
came to our house last week;
a volunteer driver brought him.

He came to show Margaret
how to harness
her remaining sight
and manage everyday living.

Told her how to tell coins from each other:
rub the penny
and smell copper on your fingers,
feel the nickel's smooth edges.

Told her how to see more clearly:
hold the magnifying glass
like this.

Mr. LeRoy ordered a white-and-red cane
for Margaret.
It arrived yesterday.
It's still in the envelope.

VARIETIES OF SILENCE

First thing you notice
is their determined anonymity.
Mostly they look down
as if their souls are seared
into the patch of floor
before their waiting chairs.
Eleven here this morning,
one is missing—
that old man
with the absent ear
and the pink grid
where that ear once listened.
Nobody speaks, except
today a bothered woman asks,
"Did anyone get a rash?"
Nobody answers, except
the shy pretty woman,
"I lost all my hair."
Smiling weakly,
she pulls off her wig.
She is skin bald.
Looking down again,
they lapse into silence.
A smiling nurse calls
George somebody—
his fifteen minutes
come and go.
Have a nice day,
see you tomorrow.
Odd,
a few still
radiate hope.

TRA LE, TRA LA

Thirteen rabbits happy hopping

over here, over there, over each other
which will be odd rabbit out?

Noses twitch, ears wiggle waggle
fluffy tails flip like chorus girls
—but some are boys.

None remembers—
hawks watch
wait for rabbit sandwiches.

Three interrupt nature's game
squat on weary haunches
nip tulip lunches.

To heck with vitamin C
to be or not to be
on with springtime's mating.

On with copulating
and populating
summertime gardens.

IF THE SHOE FITS

His crooked left arm
hung half limp.
He walked like a busted gyroscope
sideways, over-correcting
like a happy drunk.
His right hand, cradled close to his thigh,
clutched the way a jockey grips his whip,
a 22-inch shoe horn with a silver handle.

When the nurse called him to see the doctor,
waiting patients stared
as he rolled that mysterious shoe horn
inside his weather-worn mackinaw.

CONFUSION'S FACE

In forgetful minds
lost memories muddle with missfiled
rememberings, while what we think we
knew
already flew away to the edges
of dusty cobwebs where stuff is stored
for aging years and seldom retrieval.

We search for names and occasions.
What pops out is confused with
what we went in for in the first place.
We can't recall what it was
we were trying so hard to remember.

WALKING NOWHERE

How many trips, how many miles
around and around how many lost
worlds on their way to childish
dream places? So many journeys,
mumbling, humming,
crying, whistling. How
lost their minds. Too tired to
walk more, they find a private nap
nook to rest, sleep, sleep away
confusion, muddled memories. Not
tomorrow, not yesterday, but years
stored in disarray. Why do
they insist on holding dangling
hands, to lead them in strange
directions where there is
no future—no way back.

HOME ALONE
WITH LEFTOVERS

I'm on my knees to the gods
of home's original junk food

I'm on my knees, praying
before the fridge's open door:

two tired blushing radishes
half a limping carrot stick

Monday's soy-soaked drumstick
bottom half of English muffin

three messy meat loaf slices
no leaner weiner ever hid here

open can of fizzled Mello-yello
what happened to home-cooking

"Hello, Mark's Noontime Buffet,
still serving? I'll be right over."

VIRTUAL ALONENESS

Overwhelming crowds at The Fall Festival
numbered more than two hundred thousand,
yet only a few nodded as if in greeting.

Yellow jackets helped nibble corn on the cob,
vendors wrapped barbecued pork between
    rugged breads,
designated drivers sipped bottles of O'Douls.

Two close family friends missed greeting me.
Crowds obscured my eager presence—
    they did
not see shadows taller than their trees.

Finally, after eight blocks: a friendly face,
my name called out in warmest recognition.
Called me Richie, my dead brother's name.

MIDWIFE TO 800 HEIFERS

—for granddaughter Augusta

No honors at Harvard have prepped her
    for this,
no Mayflower heritage matches *her West.*

Yet she cherishes the rigors,
the cowhands she eats and bunks with,
the hard-swearing, hard-riding over
    60,000 acres.
She lends a hand at birthings and brandings,
brings a calm to first-birth heifers.

Surprises will hide under blankets of winter
twelve miles from Casper in Wyoming's
    wildness.
What fearless, foolhardy courage propels her?

THE PRAYING OF BIRDS

May the God of Gulls listen—
hear the hurts of harried birds

We gulls are not complaining fowl,
our cries are earthwide warnings

Polluted waters ruin our living—
the fish we need for food gasp and die

Speeding boaters disturb our housing,
mess up shorelines, send us soaring.

We screaming gulls are not just arguing
we cry, begging God to listen

Watch us serve each other, lovingly
peck mites from moulting feathers

See how we pray, standing one-legged,
worried God may miss our petitions.

LONELY OLD BARN

—for Neil and Pat McCarty

Barn full of smells,
memories of animal noises
stir forgotten senses.

Like empty-nest families,
rooms full of silence
echo loudly of loneliness.

The barn once suffered overwork,
its tasks never quite done.
Now, no one schedules a thing.

Tumbled bins have lost their life,
gutters drain only yesterdays.
A mouse whimpers for company.

Where has all the living gone?
Where now the sweat of dreams,
quiet tombstone of other days?

BROTHERS

My brother is lost
in the harsh cold wild,
my rabbit supper stales.

    I listen at the wind.

He is hunter and fighter,
stalks valleys,
reads the rise of rolling hills.

    I try not to worry—
    fear sends off scent.
    But I shiver, hair high on end.

My brother wears feathers.
His wily body hides
in the warm skin
of my father.

Crusty old ranchers
fear this brother
as they fear me.
Their lost sheep
feed and warm us.

Tomorrow I will find him,
tonight
he hides in nature

I go now
to the crest of the butte
my sniffing nose, alert ears
point,
listen
to the talking wind.

My brother
may speak comfort
to my fears,
he is a clever brave.

I am his watching brother.

THE KEY OF C

Often I am left to
the modest middle role
of the ordinary key of C.
I dream of highs for my life's harp;
to live in the key of F sharp.
Yet, days come and evenings too
when the best I can muster is B flat.

Times without number, I remember now,
it was in the middle world
of the familiar, well-loved key of C
where I performed my best,
where I knew I belonged.

MY OWN MOON

I drive south across
Hilary Creek's sleepy mouth.
My eyes leave the road,
zero in on fullest
golden May moon.
Rising reluctant
from the shimmering surface
of Bailey's Bay,
it guides my weary endless way.
Comforted, I drive,
and drive, and drive.
The moon is mine,
squat and low,
climbing, inching southerly.
I smile at my moon.
The miles pile
as the night wears on,
another hill, another hour.
Reliably, my moon climbs
its racing face,
beckoning.
Past midnight
I climb my stairs,
drained, yearning to rest.
But first I peek
at my moon,
high in the lighted sky.
I nod good night.

FIELD OF WHITE WINGS

As winter winds slowly down,
skies hang chilly gray.
The heaven is filled with chatter,
trumpeting, whistling bird-calls.

Gracefully flapping, they glide
into the wet marsh: more than
a thousand long-necked birds
from Carolina or Mexico
en route to Hudson Bay's tundra
to breed, to nest.

They dip into Shiocton's wetlands,
the field overflowing with white wings,
to feed, to rest
for tomorrow's pre-dawn takeoff.

White showboat flotilla, they float
on water, stalk, lift dripping legs,
scan their tall necks
for spring's warm breezes.

Enough tonight to hear
another whistling swan song.